This book belongs to:

_____

Learning Tree
1 2 3

Bears

By Hannah E. Glease

Illustrated by Bernard Robinson

CHERRYTREE BOOKS

Read this book and see if you can answer the questions at the end. Ask an adult or an older friend to tell you if your answers are right or to help you if you find the questions difficult. Often there is more than one answer to a question.

A Cherrytree Book

Designed and produced by
A S Publishing

First published 1990
by Cherrytree Press Ltd
a subsidiary of
The Chivers Company Ltd
Windsor Bridge Road
Bath, Avon BA2 3AX

Copyright © Cherrytree Press Ltd 1990

British Library Cataloguing in Publication Data
Glease, Hannah E.
    Bears.
    1. Bears
    I. Title II. Robinson, Bernard. III. Series
    599.74446

    ISBN 0-7451-5085-3

Printed and bound in Italy by L.E.G.O. s.p.a., Vicenza

American brown bears

This is a big brown bear and her two cubs.
See how furry they are.
See how long their claws are.
Can you think why they have long claws?

3

There are many different kinds of bears.
Some of them look sweet and cuddly.
But they are all fierce.
Bears cannot see or hear well.
They use their noses to find food.

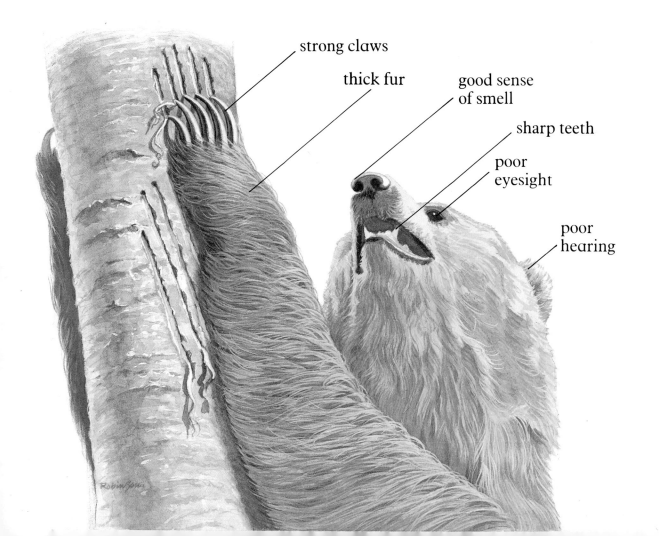

strong claws

thick fur

good sense of smell

sharp teeth

poor eyesight

poor hearing

Bears use their claws to catch their food.
Their claws also help them grip the ground.
Bears like to eat other animals.
They are so strong, they can kill with one blow
of a paw.

Some bears catch fish.
They flip the slippery fish out of the water
with their claws.
They hold the fish in their jaws.

Bears do not only eat meat.
They eat nuts and berries and mushrooms.
If they find a bees' nest, they eat the honey.
There are lots of nuts and berries in autumn.

Before winter comes, brown bears eat plenty
of food and grow fat.
In their country, it is very cold in winter and
food is hard to find.
The best thing for a bear to do is sleep.

This bear has found a hollow under the ground.
She has filled it with leaves to make a den.

The bear will sleep in her warm den for most
of the time until spring.

9

In spring, bears have their cubs.
This mother bear has two cubs.
She feeds them on milk from her body.
The cubs suck the milk from their mother.

When the cubs are older, they go out of the
den to play.
They like to chase birds and butterflies.
They enjoy fighting with each other, but they
do not hurt each other.

Playing at fighting helps the little bears learn how to look after themselves when they grow up. These two grizzly bears are fighting each other for the same fish.

American grizzly bears

American black bears

There is enough food in this litter bin for both these small black bears.
Eating scraps that people have thrown away is easier than catching their own food.

These big white bears are called polar bears.
Polar bears live in the Arctic.
It is cold and icy there all year round.
The bears swim in the sea to catch fish.

polar bears

Their thick coats keep them warm.
The fur is oily and waterproof.
The people of the Arctic catch fish, too.
They fish from boats.

15

This is a sloth bear and her cubs.
She is eating little insects called termites.
She has broken open their nest with her long claws.
She uses her long snout to suck out all the insects.
Sloth bears are sometimes called honey bears
because they like to eat honey.

Asian sloth bear

South American
spectacled bear

This is a spectacled bear.
It likes to eat fruit and leaves.
It climbs tall palm trees to reach the soft stems
at the top.
Why do you think it is called a spectacled bear?

The Himalayan bear lives in the highest
mountains in the world.
When the sun comes out, it likes to sunbathe.
It is cold in the mountains, so it makes a
carpet of leaves on the snowy ground.

Himalayan bears

Asian sun bears

These little sun bears are good climbers.
They make beds high in the trees.
They sunbathe or sleep in them during the day.
At night they go out hunting.

Long ago people used to tame bears.
They led them on a chain and made them dance.
People liked to watch them dancing.
Sometimes they set dogs on them to bait them.
They did not know how cruel it was.

More about bears

Once bears lived over the whole of Europe. Now they live only in the the Arctic and in northern Europe, North America, South America and Asia. There are no wild bears in Africa, Australia or Antarctica.

There are eight kinds of bear.
Brown bears These include Kodiak, Alaskan, European and Asian brown bears.

Polar bears These are the second largest bears and the strongest swimmers.

Grizzly bears Grizzlies are very fierce bears that live in North America. Their fur has silver tips that make it look 'grizzled'.

American black bears live in the forests of North America. They can run very fast.

Asian black bears, including Himalayan bears, are also called moon bears because of the crescent-shaped marking on their chest.

Sloth bears are middle-sized bears that live in Asia.

Spectacled bears live in the mountain forests of South America.

Sun bears are the smallest bears. They live in Asia and are sometimes called Malayan bears. They are called sun bears because of the marking on their chest.

The largest bears are Alaskan brown bears (weight 500 kilograms, height 2.7 metres). Sun bears are the smallest (weight 68 kilograms, height 1.2 metres).

Bears are so strong that they can kill almost any other animal. They can run fast to catch their prey. They can easily hurt or kill people, so it is never safe to go near them.

Cubs stay with their mother for about two years. They live to between 15 and 30 years of age.

1

1 What are baby bears called?

2 What do bears get from bees?

3 What is a bear's nest called?

4 Why are bears dangerous?

5 What do newborn cubs feed on?

6 What do human babies feed on?

7 Can you draw a picture of a bear?

2

8 Make a nature notebook. Put your drawings and the answers to these questions in it. Think of other questions to ask about bears. Put those in your notebook, too.

9 Why do you think polar bears are white?

10 Can bears swim?

11 Name one kind of bear that catches fish.

12 What is a bear's coat like?

13 Do bears always walk on all fours?

14 Name three things that bears like to eat.

15 What do bears use their long claws for?

16 Can bears climb trees?

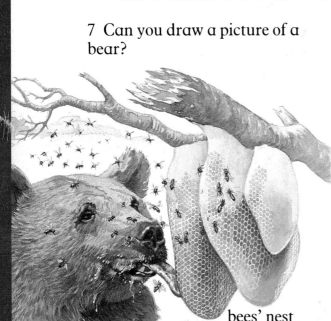

bees' nest

3

17 What kind of animals are termites? Are they insects, mammals or birds?

18 How long is a bear's tail?

19 Polar bears live in the Arctic. What kind of bears live in the Antarctic?

20 What kind of bear lives in South America?

21 Where would you find a sun bear? Where would you find a moon bear?

22 What colours can bears be?

23 How does a bear last through the winter without starving?

24 What does the sloth bear use its long snout for?

25 What do young bears learn by playing at fighting?

26 Can you guess if a full grown polar bear would be:
heavier than you?
heavier than a pony?
heavier than an elephant?

27 Can you write or tell a story about a bear?

28 Bruin is a famous name for a bear. Can you find out what the word Bruin means?

29 When you have understood everything about bears in this book, you may want to find out more about bears. Where will you find more books about bears?

30 Bears have fewer and fewer wild places to live in. Can you think why?

31 When a bear eats honey, the bees get angry. Do you think that they sting the bear? Does the bear mind if they do?

Index